Practical
Chinese

p^3

This is a P³ Book
This edition published in 2003

P³
Queen Street House
4 Queen Street
Bath BA1 1HE, UK

ISBN: 1-40540-547-3

Printed in China

NOTE

This book uses metric and imperial measurements. Follow the same units
of measurement throughout; do not mix metric and imperial.
All spoon measurements are level: teaspoons are assumed to be 5 ml, and
tablespoons are assumed to be 15 ml. Unless otherwise stated,
milk is assumed to be full fat, eggs and individual vegetables such as potatoes
are medium, and pepper is freshly ground black pepper.

The nutritional information provided for each recipe is per serving or per person.
Optional ingredients, variations or serving suggestions have
not been included in the calculations. The times given for each recipe are an approximate
guide only because the preparation times may differ according to the techniques used by
different people and the cooking times may vary as a result of the type of oven used.

Recipes using raw or very lightly cooked eggs should be
avoided by children, the elderly, pregnant women, convalescents,
and anyone suffering from an illness.

Contents

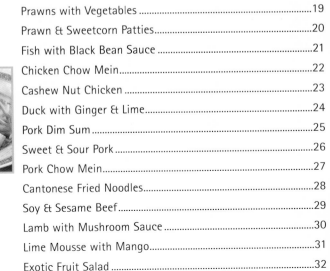

Introduction

The abundance of Chinese restaurants in the West demonstrates perfectly the popularity of Chinese cooking. Authentic dishes from all over China are assembled here for you to try at home. These recipes are delicious, incredibly easy to prepare and, fortunately, for those with a busy lifestyle, many can be cooked in under an hour.

The arrival of Chinese cuisine

Chinese cuisine was introduced to the West when Chinese migrants settled in San Francisco during the Gold Rush. Since then, Chinese restaurants have spread throughout the world and Chinese ingredients and cooking equipment are now readily available.

Benefits of eating Chinese food

Chinese food is generally cooked rapidly over a very high heat, using a minimum of oil, which preserves texture, flavour and nutrients. The ingredients include fish, vegetables and meats combined with noodles or rice, which are excellent sources of slow, energy-releasing carbohydrates. High-cholesterol ingredients, such as dairy products and red meats, are used sparingly, if at

all. Chinese meals are well-balanced, not only in terms of a healthy diet, but also in their aim to provide complementary courses: spicy dishes are served with sweet-and-sour alternatives, dry-cooked dishes are accompanied by those in sauces.

Regional cuisine

China is a vast country with an enormous variety of different climates, which affect the agricultural productivity within each area. The harsh climate around the capital of Beijing in the north is very different from the mild coastal areas of the south; the influence of the Yangtze river is felt strongly at its delta near Shanghai in the east, while the west enjoys a mild, humid climate and rich fertile soil in the shadow of the Tien Shan mountains. The regional cuisines are equally diverse.

The north: dishes from the north are strongly flavoured, using leeks, onions and garlic. Many dishes contain lamb, not pork, bearing testimony to the Moslem culture introduced by invading Tartars from Central Asia. In northern areas, wheat is used more frequently than rice, served as pancakes, noodles or dumplings.

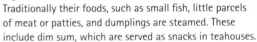

The south: the first emigrant Chinese originated from Canton and its surrounding areas; this is still the most commonly known Chinese regional food in the West. Traditionally their foods, such as small fish, little parcels of meat or patties, and dumplings are steamed. These include dim sum, which are served as snacks in teahouses.

The east: benefiting enormously from the annual flooding of the Yangtze River, the east boasts very rich soil. The fertile plains allow growth of broccoli, sweet potatoes, pak choi, soya beans, tea and rice – the list is almost endless. Many of the traditional dishes are vegetarian and they vary enormously. Today, the regional cuisines of the east have been influenced by the city of Shanghai, which has assimilated culinary influences from around the world. Dairy products have infiltrated Chinese kitchens, but duck, ham and fish in piquant spices still remain specialities.

The west: benefiting from a mild climate, Szechuan is noted for its robust, richly coloured, spicy dishes. Szechuan cooking uses lots of garlic, ginger, onions, leeks and Szechuan peppercorns. Western China is renowned for its smoking, drying, pickling and salting techniques, which are used to preserve foods and enhance flavours. Seven different ingredients are used to achieve seven very

particular flavours in Szechuan cooking: sweet flavours use honey; salty ones, soy sauce; sour flavours, vinegar; bitter ones, onions or leeks; fragrant dishes, garlic or ginger; sesame flavours, sesame seed paste; and hot recipes use chillies.

Ingredients

Chinese ingredients are widely available in supermarkets, but it is worth investing in better-quality versions of some of the oils, condiments and sauces from specialist shops.

Bamboo shoots: fresh bamboo shoots are bland on their own but are used for their texture. Remove tough outer skins, then boil in water for 40–50 minutes.

Bean sauce: available in cans or jars, this savoury paste is black or yellow and made from crushed, salted soya beans, flour and four spices. Red paste is used for sweet sauces.

Chillies: fiery-hot chilli oil contains chilli flakes and needs to be used with caution. Chilli bean sauce contains soya beans and uses the chillies for flavour – it should also be used sparingly. If using fresh chillies, remember that small, pointed chillies are much hotter than larger, more rounded

ones. Parts containing seeds are the hottest, so removing these will reduce the potency of the chillies.

Chinese five-spice: the five spices are fennel seeds, cinnamon, cloves, star anise and Szechuan pepper. They produce a musty, pungent aroma and add a delicious, distinctive flavour.

Chinese rice wine and vinegar: rice wine is made from glutinous rice and resembles dry sherry (which can be used as a suitable alternative in Chinese cooking). Rice vinegar is distilled from Chinese rice wine and is stronger than red vinegar. Cider vinegar or white wine vinegar can be used instead.

Dried mushrooms: shiitake mushrooms have a strong flavour; they are expensive but a little goes a long way.

The dried mushrooms need to be soaked for 20–30 minutes before use; the water can be kept for stock.

Ginger: root ginger can be bought in the supermarket: look for plump pieces with shiny, unblemished skin. Cut the amount you need, peel it, then chop, slice or grate it. Fresh ginger will keep for weeks in a cool, dry place. Ground ginger is not a good substitute.

Hoisin sauce: made from soya beans, sugar, flour, vinegar, chillies, garlic, sesame oil and salt. It is used for flavouring in small quantities combined with soy sauce or used alone on duck, spare ribs or seafood.

Lemon grass: the lower part of lemon grass stalks add a slightly citrus flavour to a dish. If used whole, lemon grass should be removed before serving.

Star anise: this is a star-shaped fruit with a strong aniseed flavour. It is usually used ground. Pods can also be used but they should be removed before serving.

Cooking equipment

A good-quality wok is essential if you want to achieve an authentic Chinese taste. Traditionally made from cast iron, there are now many different types of wok. Stainless steel woks are not recommended, however, because they scorch, and some non-stick woks cannot tolerate the very high temperatures required. To cook food evenly, it should be tossed or stirred continuously. There are few special tools required for Chinese cooking. A lid for your wok is essential for steaming. Cleavers are used to chop, dice and cut everything from shellfish and herbs to meat and vegetables. Chopsticks are used for preparation – they are unlikely to damage delicate food – as well as for eating.

KEY		
	Simplicity level 1–3 (1 easiest, 3 slightly harder)	
	Preparation time	
	Cooking time	

Mushroom Noodle Soup

A light, refreshing, clear soup of mushrooms, cucumber and small pieces of rice noodles, flavoured with soy sauce and a touch of garlic.

NUTRITIONAL INFORMATION

Calories	84	Sugars	.........1g
Protein	.........1g	Fat	...........8g
Carbohydrate	....3g	Saturates	.......1g

 5 mins   10 mins

SERVES 4

I N G R E D I E N T S

125 g/4½ oz flat or open-cup mushrooms

½ cucumber

2 spring onions

1 garlic clove

2 tbsp vegetable oil

25 g/1 oz Chinese rice noodles

¾ tsp salt

1 tbsp soy sauce

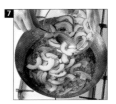

1 Wash the mushrooms and pat dry on kitchen paper. Slice thinly. Do not peel them because this adds more flavour.

2 Halve the cucumber lengthways. Using a teaspoon, scoop out the seeds, and slice the cucumber thinly.

COOK'S TIP

Scooping out the seeds from the cucumber gives it a prettier effect when sliced, and also helps to reduce any bitterness, but if you prefer, you can leave them in.

3 Finely chop the spring onions and cut the garlic clove into thin strips.

4 Heat the vegetable oil in a large frying pan or wok.

5 Add the chopped spring onions and garlic strips to the pan or wok and then stir-fry them for 30 seconds. Add the thinly sliced mushrooms and stir-fry for 2–3 minutes.

6 Stir in 600 ml/1 pint water. Break the noodles into short lengths and add them to the soup. Bring the soup to the boil, stirring occasionally.

7 Add the cucumber slices, salt and soy sauce and simmer for 2–3 minutes.

8 Serve the mushroom noodle soup in warmed bowls, distributing the noodles and vegetables evenly.

Chicken & Sweetcorn Soup

This warming, creamy chicken soup is made into a meal in itself with the addition of strands of vermicelli.

NUTRITIONAL INFORMATION

Calories 401   Sugars 6g
Protein . . . . 31g   Fat 24g
Carbohydrate . . . 17g   Saturates 13g

5 mins   25 mins

SERVES 4

I N G R E D I E N T S

450 g/1 lb boned chicken breasts, cut into strips

1.2 litres/2 pints chicken stock

150 ml/5 fl oz double cream

100 g /3½ oz dried vermicelli

1 tbsp cornflour

3 tbsp milk

175 g/6 oz sweetcorn

salt and pepper

1 Put the chicken strips, stock and double cream into a large saucepan and bring to the boil over a low heat. Lower the heat slightly and then simmer for about 20 minutes. Season the soup with salt and pepper to taste.

2 Meanwhile, cook the vermicelli in lightly salted boiling water for about 10–12 minutes or until just tender. Drain the pasta and keep warm.

3 In a small bowl, mix together the cornflour and milk to make a smooth paste. Stir the cornflour mixture into the soup until it has thickened.

4 Add the sweetcorn and vermicelli to the pan and heat through.

5 Transfer the soup to a warm serving bowl or individual soup bowls and serve immediately.

COOK'S TIP

If you are short of time, buy ready-cooked chicken, remove any skin and cut it into slices.

Chinese Potato & Pork Soup

In this recipe the pork is seasoned with traditional Chinese flavourings – soy sauce, rice wine vinegar and a dash of sesame oil.

NUTRITIONAL INFORMATION

Calories 166	Sugars 2g
Protein 10g	Fat 5g
Carbohydrate ...26g	Saturates 1g

5 mins   20 mins

SERVES 4

I N G R E D I E N T S

1 litre/1¾ pints chicken stock

2 large potatoes, peeled and diced

2 tbsp rice wine vinegar

2 tbsp cornflour

4 tbsp water

125 g/4½ oz pork fillet, sliced

1 tbsp light soy sauce

1 tsp sesame oil

1 carrot, cut into thin strips

1 tsp chopped fresh root ginger

3 spring onions, thinly sliced

1 red pepper, deseeded and sliced

225 g/8 oz canned bamboo shoots, drained

1 Add the chicken stock, diced potatoes and 1 tablespoon of the rice wine vinegar to a saucepan and bring to the boil. Lower the heat until just simmering.

2 Mix the cornflour with the water, then stir into the hot stock.

3 Bring the stock back to the boil, stirring until thickened, then lower the heat until it is just simmering again.

4 Put the pork slices in a dish and mix with the remaining rice wine vinegar, the soy sauce and the sesame oil.

5 Add the pork slices and their liquid to the stock along with the carrot and ginger. Cook for 10 minutes. Stir in the spring onions, red pepper and bamboo shoots. Cook for another 5 minutes. Pour the soup into warmed bowls and then serve immediately.

VARIATION

For extra heat, add 1 chopped red chilli or 1 teaspoon of chilli powder to the soup in step 5.

Asparagus Parcels

These small parcels are ideal as part of a main meal and irresistible as a quick snack with extra plum sauce for dipping.

NUTRITIONAL INFORMATION

Calories 194   Sugars 2g
Protein ....3g   Fat 16g
Carbohydrate ....11g Saturates 4g

 5 mins   25 mins

SERVES 4

I N G R E D I E N T S

100 g/3½ oz fine-tipped asparagus

1 red pepper, deseeded and thinly sliced

35 g/1¼ oz beansprouts

2 tbsp plum sauce

1 egg yolk

8 sheets filo pastry

oil, for deep-frying

1 Place the asparagus, red pepper and beansprouts in a large mixing bowl.

2 Add the plum sauce to the vegetables and mix until well combined.

3 Beat the egg yolk in a bowl and set aside until required.

4 Lay the sheets of filo pastry out on a clean work surface.

5 Place a little of the asparagus and red pepper filling at the top end of each filo pastry sheet. Brush the edges of the filo pastry sheets with a little of the beaten egg yolk.

6 Roll up the filo pastry, tucking in the ends and enclosing the filling like a spring roll. Repeat with the remaining filo sheets.

7 Heat the oil for deep-frying in a large preheated wok. Carefully cook the parcels, 2 at a time, in the hot oil for 4–5 minutes or until crispy.

8 Remove the cooked parcels with a slotted spoon and leave to drain on kitchen paper.

9 Transfer the parcels to warm serving plates and serve immediately.

COOK'S TIP
Be sure to use fine-tipped asparagus because it is more tender than the larger stems.

Son-in-Law Eggs

This recipe is supposedly so called because it is an easy dish for a son-in-law to cook to impress his new mother-in-law!

NUTRITIONAL INFORMATION

Calories . . . . . . .229 Sugars 8g
Protein . . . . .9g Fat 18g
Carbohydrate . . . .8g Saturates 3g

🍲 15 mins   🕐 15 mins

SERVES 4

I N G R E D I E N T S

6 hard-boiled eggs

4 tbsp sunflower oil

1 onion, thinly sliced

2 fresh red chillies, deseeded and sliced

2 tbsp sugar

1 tbsp water

2 tsp tamarind pulp

1 tbsp liquid seasoning, such as Maggi

freshly cooked rice, to serve

1 Shell the hard-boiled eggs and then prick each one 2 or 3 times with a cocktail stick.

2 Heat the sunflower oil in a wok and add the eggs. Cook them in the wok until crispy and golden. Drain the eggs on absorbent kitchen paper.

3 Halve the eggs lengthways and put them on a serving dish.

4 Reserve one tablespoon of the oil, drain off the rest, then heat the reserved tablespoonful in the wok. Cook the sliced onion and chillies over a high heat until golden and slightly crisp. Drain on kitchen paper.

5 Heat the sugar, water, tamarind pulp and liquid seasoning in the wok and simmer for 5 minutes until thickened.

6 Pour the sauce over the eggs and spoon over the onion and chillies. Serve immediately with cooked rice.

COOK'S TIP

Tamarind pulp is sold in Oriental stores, and is quite sour. If it is not available, use twice the amount of lemon juice in its place.

Oriental Salad

This colourful, crisp salad has a fresh orange dressing and is topped with crunchy vermicelli.

NUTRITIONAL INFORMATION

Calories 139	Sugars 8g	
Protein 5g	Fat 7g	
Carbohydrate ...15g	Saturates 1g	

10 mins   5 mins

SERVES 4

I N G R E D I E N T S

25 g/1 oz dried vermicelli

½ head Chinese leaves

125 g/4½ oz beansprouts

6 radishes

125 g/4½ oz mangetouts

1 large carrot

125 g/4½ oz sprouting beans

D R E S S I N G

juice of 1 orange

1 tbsp sesame seeds, toasted

1 tsp honey

1 tsp sesame oil

1 tbsp hazelnut oil

1 Break the vermicelli into small strands. Heat a wok and cook the vermicelli in the dry pan until lightly golden.

2 Remove from the pan with a slotted spoon and set aside until required.

3 Using a sharp knife or food processor, shred the Chinese leaves and rinse with the beansprouts. Drain thoroughly and place the leaves and beansprouts in a large mixing bowl.

4 Thinly slice the radishes. Trim the mangetouts and cut each into 3 pieces.

Cut the carrot into thin matchsticks. Add the sprouting beans and prepared vegetables to the bowl.

5 Place all the dressing ingredients in a screw-top jar and shake well. Pour over the salad and toss together.

6 Transfer the salad to a serving bowl and sprinkle over the crispy vermicelli before serving.

COOK'S TIP

Make your own sprouting beans by soaking mung and aduki beans overnight in cold water; drain and rinse. Place in a large jar covered with muslin to secure it. Lay the jar on its side and place in indirect light. For the next 3 days, rinse the beans once each day in cold water until ready to eat.

Beansprout Salad

This is a very light dish and is ideal on its own for a summer meal or as a starter.

NUTRITIONAL INFORMATION

Calories 70   Sugars 5g
Protein . . . . .4g   Fat 3g
Carbohydrate . . . .7g   Saturates 0.5g

 10 mins   ⏱ 5 mins

SERVES 4

I N G R E D I E N T S

1 green pepper, deseeded

1 carrot

1 celery stalk

2 tomatoes

350 g/12 oz beansprouts

1 small cucumber

1 garlic clove, crushed

dash of chilli sauce

2 tbsp light soy sauce

1 tsp wine vinegar

2 tsp sesame oil

16 fresh chives

1 Using a sharp knife, cut the green pepper, carrot and celery into matchsticks and then finely chop the tomatoes.

2 Blanch the beansprouts in boiling water for 1 minute. Drain well and rinse under cold water. Drain them again thoroughly.

3 Cut the cucumber in half lengthways. Scoop out the seeds with a teaspoon and discard them. Cut the flesh into matchsticks.

4 Mix the cucumber with the beansprouts, green pepper, carrot, tomatoes and celery.

5 To make the dressing, mix together the garlic, chilli sauce, soy sauce, wine vinegar and sesame oil in a small bowl.

6 Pour the dressing over the vegetables, tossing together until well coated.

7 Spoon the beansprout salad into a serving dish or onto 4 individual serving plates. Garnish the salad with fresh chives and serve.

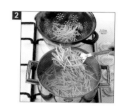

VARIATION

Substitute 350 g/12 oz cooked, cooled French beans or mangetouts for the cucumber. Vary the beansprouts for a different flavour. Try aduki bean or alfalfa sprouts, as well as the better-known mung and soya bean sprouts.

Crispy Seaweed

This tasty Chinese starter is not all that it seems – the 'seaweed' is in fact pak choi, which is then cooked, salted and tossed with pine kernels.

NUTRITIONAL INFORMATION

Calories 214   Sugars 14g
Protein . . . . .6g   Fat 15g
Carbohydrate . . .15g   Saturates 2g

 10 mins   5 mins

SERVES 4

I N G R E D I E N T S

1 kg/2 lb 4 oz pak choi

850 ml/1½ pints groundnut oil, for deep-frying

1 tsp salt

1 tbsp caster sugar

2½ tbsp pine kernels, toasted

1 Rinse the pak choi leaves under cold running water and then pat dry thoroughly with kitchen paper.

2 Discarding any tough outer leaves, roll up each pak choi leaf, then slice through thinly so that the leaves are finely shredded. Alternatively, use a food processor to shred the pak choi.

3 Heat the groundnut oil in a large wok or heavy-based frying pan.

4 Carefully add the shredded pak choi leaves to the wok or frying pan and cook for about 30 seconds or until they shrivel up and become crispy (you will probably need to do this in several batches, depending on the size of your wok).

5 Use a sieve or slotted spoon to lift out the crispy seaweed from the wok and drain on kitchen paper.

6 Transfer the crispy seaweed to a large bowl and toss with the salt, sugar and pine kernels. Serve immediately on warm serving plates.

COOK'S TIP

The tough, outer leaves of pak choi are discarded because these will spoil the overall taste and texture of the dish. If pak choi is unavailable, use savoy cabbage instead, drying the leaves thoroughly before cooking.

Chinese Leaves in Honey

Chinese leaves are somewhat similar to lettuce in that the leaves are delicate with a sweet flavour.

NUTRITIONAL INFORMATION

Calories 121	Sugars 6g
Protein 5g	Fat 7g
Carbohydrate . . .10g	Saturates 1g

5 mins   10 mins

SERVES 4

I N G R E D I E N T S

450 g/1 lb Chinese leaves

1 tbsp groundnut oil

1 tsp grated fresh root ginger

2 garlic cloves, crushed

1 fresh red chilli, deseeded and sliced

1 tbsp Chinese rice wine or dry sherry

4½ tsp light soy sauce

1 tbsp clear honey

125 ml/4 fl oz orange juice

1 tbsp sesame oil

2 tsp sesame seeds

strips of orange zest, to garnish

COOK'S TIP

Single-flower honey has a better, more individual flavour than blended honey. Acacia honey is typically Chinese, but you could also try clover, lemon blossom, lime flower or orange blossom honey.

1 Separate the Chinese leaves and shred them finely, using a sharp knife.

2 Heat the groundnut oil in a preheated wok. Add the ginger, garlic and chilli to the wok and cook the mixture for about 30 seconds.

3 Add the Chinese leaves, Chinese rice wine or sherry, soy sauce, honey and orange juice to the wok. Lower the heat and leave to simmer for 5 minutes.

4 Add the sesame oil to the wok, sprinkle the sesame seeds over the top and mix to combine.

5 Transfer to a warm serving dish, garnish with the orange zest and serve immediately.

Vegetable Chop Suey

Make sure that the vegetables are all cut into pieces of a similar size in this recipe, so that they cook within the same amount of time.

NUTRITIONAL INFORMATION

Calories . . . . . . .155 Sugars 6g
Protein . . . . .4g Fat 12g
Carbohydrate . . . .9g Saturates 2g

5 mins   5 mins

SERVES 4

INGREDIENTS

1 yellow pepper, deseeded

1 red pepper, deseeded

1 carrot

1 courgette

1 fennel bulb

1 onion

60 g/2 oz mangetouts

2 tbsp groundnut oil

3 garlic cloves, crushed

1 tsp grated fresh root ginger

125 g/4½ oz beansprouts

2 tsp light brown sugar

2 tbsp light soy sauce

125 ml/4 fl oz vegetable stock

 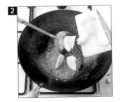 

1 Cut the peppers, carrot, courgette and fennel into thin slices. Cut the onion into quarters, then cut each quarter in half. Slice the mangetouts diagonally to create the maximum surface area.

2 Heat the oil in a preheated wok, add the garlic and ginger and cook for 30 seconds. Add the onion and cook for another 30 seconds.

3 Add the peppers, carrot, courgette, fennel and mangetouts to the wok and cook for 2 minutes.

4 Add the beansprouts to the wok and stir in the sugar, soy sauce and stock. Reduce the heat to low and simmer for about 1–2 minutes until the vegetables are tender and coated in the sauce.

5 Transfer the vegetables and sauce to a serving dish and serve immediately.

VARIATION
Use any combination of colourful vegetables that you have to hand to make this versatile dish.

Bamboo with Spinach

In this recipe, spinach is cooked with spices and then braised in a soy-flavoured sauce with bamboo shoots for a rich, delicious dish.

NUTRITIONAL INFORMATION

Calories	105	Sugars	. . . . .1g
Protein	. . . . .3g	Fat	. . . . .9g
Carbohydrate	. . . .3g	Saturates	. . . . . . .2g

5 mins   10 mins

SERVES 4

I N G R E D I E N T S

3 tbsp groundnut oil

225 g/8 oz spinach, chopped

175 g/6 oz canned bamboo shoots, drained and rinsed

1 garlic clove, crushed

2 fresh red chillies, sliced

pinch of ground cinnamon

300 ml/10 fl oz vegetable stock

pinch of sugar

pinch of salt

1 tbsp light soy sauce

1 tsp cornflour (optional)

COOK'S TIP

Fresh bamboo shoots are rarely available in the West and, in any case, are extremely time-consuming to prepare. Canned bamboo shoots are quite satisfactory, because they are used for their crunchy texture, not their flavour, which is fairly insipid.

1 Heat the groundnut oil in a preheated wok or large frying pan, swirling the oil around the bottom of the wok until it is really hot.

2 Add the spinach and bamboo shoots to the wok and cook for 1 minute.

3 Add the garlic, chillies and cinnamon to the mixture in the wok and cook for another 30 seconds.

4 Stir in the stock, sugar, salt and light soy sauce, cover and cook over a medium heat for 5 minutes or until the vegetables are cooked through and the sauce has reduced. If there is too much cooking liquid, blend 1 teaspoon of cornflour with 2 teaspoons of cold water and stir into the sauce.

5 Transfer the bamboo shoots and spinach to a serving dish and serve.

Chatuchak Fried Rice

An excellent way to use up leftover rice. Pop it in the freezer as soon as it is cool, and it will be ready to reheat at any time.

NUTRITIONAL INFORMATION

Calories 241	Sugars 5g
Protein 7g	Fat 5g
Carbohydrate . . .46g	Saturates 1g

🍲 25 mins   🕐 15 mins

SERVES 4

I N G R E D I E N T S

1 tbsp sunflower oil

3 shallots, finely chopped

2 garlic cloves, crushed

1 red chilli, deseeded and finely chopped

2.5-cm/1-inch piece root ginger, finely shredded

½ green pepper, deseeded and finely sliced

150 g/5½ oz baby aubergines, cut into quarters

90 g/3¼ oz sugar snap peas or mangetouts, trimmed and blanched

90 g/3¼ oz baby corn, halved lengthways and blanched

1 tomato, cut into 8 pieces

90 g/3¼ oz beansprouts

500 g/1 lb 2 oz cooked jasmine rice

2 tbsp tomato ketchup

2 tbsp light soy sauce

T O   G A R N I S H

fresh coriander leaves

lime wedges

1 Heat the sunflower oil in a wok or large, heavy frying pan over a high heat.

2 Add the shallots, garlic, chilli and ginger to the wok or frying pan. Stir until the shallots have softened.

3 Add the green pepper and baby aubergines to the pan and stir well.

4 Add the sugar snap peas or mangetouts, baby corn, tomato and beansprouts. Stir-fry for 3 minutes.

5 Add the cooked jasmine rice to the wok, and lift and stir with two spoons for 4–5 minutes until no more steam is released.

6 Stir the tomato ketchup and soy sauce into the mixture in the wok.

7 Serve the rice immediately, garnished with sprigs of fresh coriander and lime wedges for squeezing over the rice.

Chinese Omelette

This omelette contains chicken and prawns. It is cooked as a whole omelette and then sliced for serving as part of a Chinese meal.

NUTRITIONAL INFORMATION

Calories 309	Sugars 0g
Protein 34g	Fat 19g
Carbohydrate ...0.2g	Saturates 5g

 5 mins   5 mins

SERVES 4

I N G R E D I E N T S

8 eggs

225 g/8 oz cooked chicken, shredded

12 tiger prawns, peeled and deveined

2 tbsp chopped fresh chives

2 tsp light soy sauce

dash of chilli sauce

2 tbsp vegetable oil

VARIATION

You could add extra flavour to the omelette by stirring in 3 tablespoons of finely chopped fresh coriander or 1 teaspoon of sesame seeds with the chives in step 2.

1 Lightly beat the eggs in a large mixing bowl. Add the shredded chicken and tiger prawns and mix well.

2 Stir in the chopped chives, light soy sauce and chilli sauce, mixing well to combine all the ingredients.

3 Heat the vegetable oil in a large, heavy-based frying pan over a medium heat. Pour in the egg mixture,

tilting the pan to coat the base evenly and completely. Cook the eggs over a medium heat, gently stirring the omelette with a fork to let the raw egg run underneath the set egg, until the surface is just set and the underside is a golden-brown colour.

4 When the omelette is set, slide it out of the pan with the aid of a palette knife. Cut the Chinese omelette into squares or slices and serve immediately.

Prawns with Vegetables

This colourful and delicious dish is cooked with vegetables: vary them according to seasonal availability.

NUTRITIONAL INFORMATION

Calories 298   Sugars 1g
Protein ....13g   Fat 26g
Carbohydrate ....3g   Saturates 3g

5 mins   10 mins

SERVES 4

INGREDIENTS

60 g/2¼ oz mangetouts

½ small carrot

60 g/2¼ oz baby corn

60 g/2¼ oz straw mushrooms

6–9 oz/175–250 g raw tiger prawns, peeled

1 tsp salt

½ egg white, lightly beaten

1 tsp cornflour

300 ml/10 fl oz vegetable oil

1 spring onion, cut into short sections

4 slices root ginger, peeled and finely chopped

½ tsp sugar

1 tbsp light soy sauce

1 tsp Chinese rice wine or dry sherry

a few drops of sesame oil

TO GARNISH

lemon slices

fresh chives

1 Using a sharp knife, top and tail the mangetouts. Cut the carrot into the same size as the mangetouts. Halve the baby corn and straw mushrooms.

2 Put the prawns, a pinch of the salt, and the egg white into a bowl. Mix the cornflour with 2 teaspoons of water and add to the bowl. Mix together until the prawns are evenly coated.

3 Preheat a wok over a high heat for 2–3 minutes, then add the vegetable oil and heat it to medium-hot.

4 Add the prawns to the wok, stirring to separate them. Remove the prawns with a slotted spoon as soon as their colour changes.

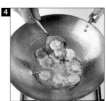

5 Pour off the oil, leaving about 1 tablespoon in the wok. Add the mangetouts, carrot, corn, mushrooms and spring onions. Then add the prawns, together with the ginger, sugar, soy sauce, and rice wine or sherry and blend well.

6 Sprinkle over the sesame oil and serve hot, garnished with lemon slices and fresh chives.

Prawn & Sweetcorn Patties

Chopped small prawns and sweetcorn are combined in a light batter, which is dropped in spoonfuls into hot fat to make these tasty patties.

NUTRITIONAL INFORMATION

Calories 250   Sugars 1g
Protein ....17g   Fat 9g
Carbohydrate ...26g   Saturates 2g

35 mins   20 mins

SERVES 4

I N G R E D I E N T S

125 g/4½ oz plain flour

1½ tsp baking powder

½ tsp salt

2 eggs

about 250 ml/9 fl oz cold water

1 garlic clove, very finely chopped

3 spring onions, trimmed and very finely chopped

250 g/9 oz peeled small prawns, chopped

125 g/4½ oz canned sweetcorn, drained

vegetable oil, for cooking

pepper

TO GARNISH

spring onion tassels (see Cook's Tip, below)

chilli flowers (see Cook's Tip, below)

slices of fresh lime

COOK'S TIP

To make a spring onion tassel or chilli flower, hold the stem and make slits almost down its full length several times with a sharp knife. Place in iced water to make it fan out. Remove any chilli seeds.

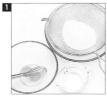  

1 Sift the flour, baking powder and ½ teaspoon salt into a bowl. Add the eggs and half the water and beat to make a smooth batter, adding extra water to give the consistency of double cream. Add the garlic and spring onions. Cover and set aside for 30 minutes.

2 Stir the prawns and sweetcorn into the batter. Season with pepper.

3 Heat 2–3 tablespoons of oil in a wok. Drop tablespoonfuls of the batter into the wok and cook over a medium heat until bubbles rise and the surface just sets. Flip the patties over and cook them on the other side until golden brown. Drain on kitchen paper.

4 Cook the remaining batter in the same way, adding more oil to the wok as required. Garnish with the spring onion tassels, chilli flowers and slices of fresh lime and serve at once.

Fish with Black Bean Sauce

Steaming is one of the preferred methods of cooking whole fish in China because it maintains both the flavour and the texture.

NUTRITIONAL INFORMATION

Calories	292	Sugars	.........3g
Protein	........44g	Fat	...........7g
Carbohydrate	....6g	Saturates	.....0.4g

 10 mins   10 mins

SERVES 4

INGREDIENTS

900 g/2 lb whole snapper, cleaned and scaled

3 garlic cloves, crushed

2 tbsp black bean sauce

1 tsp cornflour

2 tsp sesame oil

2 tbsp light soy sauce

2 tsp caster sugar

2 tbsp dry sherry

1 leek, shredded

1 small red pepper, deseeded and cut into thin strips

lemon wedges, to garnish

boiled rice or noodles, to serve

1 Rinse the fish inside and out with cold running water and pat dry with kitchen paper.

2 Make 2–3 diagonal slashes in the flesh on each side of the fish, using a sharp knife. Rub the garlic into the fish.

3 Combine the black bean sauce, cornflour, sesame oil, light soy sauce, sugar, and dry sherry in a bowl.

4 Place the fish in a shallow, heatproof dish and pour the sauce mixture over the top. Sprinkle the shredded leek (reserve some for garnish) and red pepper strips on top of the sauce.

5 Place the dish in the top of a steamer, cover and steam for 10 minutes or until the fish is cooked through.

6 Transfer the fish to a serving dish, garnish with shredded leek and lemon wedges and serve with rice or noodles.

COOK'S TIP
Insert the point of a sharp knife into the fish to test if it is cooked. If the knife goes into the flesh easily, the fish is cooked through.

Chicken Chow Mein

This classic dish requires no introduction because it is already a favourite among many people in the West.

NUTRITIONAL INFORMATION

Calories	230	Sugars 2g
Protein	........19g	Fat 11g
Carbohydrate	...14g	Saturates 2g

🥄 5 mins   🕐 20 mins

SERVES 4

I N G R E D I E N T S

250 g/9 oz medium egg noodles

2 tbsp sunflower oil

275 g/9½ oz cooked chicken breasts, shredded

1 garlic clove, finely chopped

1 red pepper, deseeded and thinly sliced

100 g/3½ oz shiitake mushrooms, sliced

6 spring onions, sliced

60 g/2¼ oz beansprouts

3 tbsp soy sauce

1 tbsp sesame oil

1 Place the egg noodles in a large, heatproof bowl or dish and break them up slightly. Pour over enough boiling water to cover the noodles and leave to stand.

2 Heat the sunflower oil in a large, preheated wok or frying pan. Add the shredded chicken, finely chopped garlic, red pepper slices, mushrooms, spring onions and beansprouts to the pan and cook for about 5 minutes.

3 Drain the noodles thoroughly. Add the noodles to the pan, toss well and cook for another 5 minutes.

4 Drizzle the soy sauce and sesame oil over the chow mein and toss until well combined.

5 Remove the chicken chow mein from the heat, transfer to warm serving bowls and serve immediately.

  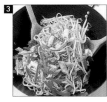

VARIATION

You can make the chow mein with a selection of vegetables for a vegetarian dish, if you prefer.

Cashew Nut Chicken

Yellow bean sauce is available from large supermarkets. Try to buy a chunky sauce instead of a smooth sauce for added texture.

NUTRITIONAL INFORMATION

Calories 398	Sugars 2g
Protein 31g	Fat 27g
Carbohydrate 8g	Saturates 4g

10 mins   15 mins

SERVES 4

INGREDIENTS

450 g/1 lb boneless chicken breasts

2 tbsp vegetable oil

1 red onion, sliced

175 g/6 oz flat mushrooms, sliced

100 g/3½ oz cashew nuts

75 g/2 ¾ oz yellow bean sauce

fresh coriander, chopped, to garnish

egg fried rice or plain boiled rice,
   to serve

1 Using a sharp knife, remove the excess skin from the chicken breasts, if desired. Cut the chicken into small, bite-sized chunks.

2 Heat the vegetable oil in a preheated wok or frying pan.

3 Add the chicken to the wok and stir-fry for 5 minutes.

4 Add the red onion and mushrooms to the wok and continue to stir-fry for another 5 minutes.

5 Place the cashew nuts on a baking tray and toast under a preheated medium grill until just browning – toasting nuts brings out their flavour.

6 Toss the toasted cashew nuts into the wok together with the yellow bean sauce and heat through. Let the sauce bubble for 2–3 minutes.

7 Transfer to warm serving bowls and garnish with chopped fresh coriander. Serve hot with egg fried rice or plain boiled rice.

VARIATION

Chicken thighs could be used instead of the chicken breasts for a more economical dish.

Duck with Ginger & Lime

Just the thing for a lazy summer day – roasted duck sliced and served with a dressing made from ginger, lime juice, sesame oil and fish sauce.

NUTRITIONAL INFORMATION

Calories	529	Sugars	.........3g
Protein	........38g	Fat	..........41g
Carbohydrate	....3g	Saturates	.......6g

 20 mins 🕐 25 mins

SERVES 4

INGREDIENTS

3 boneless Barbary duck breasts, about 250 g/9 oz each

salt

DRESSING

125 ml/4 fl oz olive oil

2 tsp sesame oil

2 tbsp lime juice

grated zest and juice of 1 orange

2 tsp fish sauce

1 tbsp grated fresh root ginger

1 garlic clove, crushed

2 tsp light soy sauce

3 spring onions, finely chopped

1 tsp sugar

about 250 g/9 oz assorted salad leaves

orange slices, to garnish (optional)

1 Wash the duck breasts, dry on kitchen paper then cut in half. Prick the skin all over with a fork and season well with salt. Place the duck breasts, skin-side down, on a wire rack or trivet over a roasting tin.

2 Cook the duck in a preheated oven, 220°C/425°F/Gas Mark 7, for about 10 minutes. Turn over and cook for about 12–15 minutes or until the duck is cooked and crisp, but still pink in the centre.

3 To make the dressing, beat the olive oil and sesame oil in a non-metallic bowl, then add the lime juice, orange zest and juice, fish sauce, grated root ginger, garlic, light soy sauce, spring onions and sugar. Beat together well until the ingredients are thoroughly blended.

4 Remove the duck from the oven, leave to cool, then cut into thick slices. Add a little dressing to moisten and coat the duck.

5 To serve, arrange the salad leaves on a serving dish. Top with the duck and drizzle over the remaining dressing.

6 Garnish with orange slices, if using, then serve at once.

Pork Dim Sum

These small steamed parcels are traditionally served as a starter and are very adaptable to your favourite fillings.

NUTRITIONAL INFORMATION

Calories	478	Sugars	.........3g
Protein	........33g	Fat	..........29g
Carbohydrate	...21g	Saturates	.......9g

10 mins   15 mins

SERVES 4

I N G R E D I E N T S

400 g/14 oz minced pork

2 spring onions, chopped

50 g/1¾ oz canned bamboo shoots, drained, rinsed and chopped

1 tbsp light soy sauce

1 tbsp dry sherry

2 tsp sesame oil

2 tsp caster sugar

1 egg white, lightly beaten

4½ tsp cornflour

24 wonton wrappers

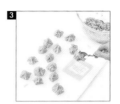

1 Place the minced pork, spring onions, bamboo shoots, soy sauce, dry sherry, sesame oil, caster sugar and beaten egg white in a large mixing bowl and mix together until all the ingredients are thoroughly combined.

2 Stir in the cornflour, mixing until thoroughly incorporated with the other ingredients.

3 Spread out the wonton wrappers on a clean work surface. Place a spoonful of the pork mixture in the centre of each wrapper and lightly brush the edges of the wrappers with water. Bring the sides of the wrappers together in the centre of the filling, pinching firmly together.

4 Line a steamer with a clean, damp tea towel and arrange the wontons inside. Cover and steam for 5–7 minutes until the dim sum are cooked through. Serve immediately.

COOK'S TIP
Bamboo steamers are designed to rest on the sloping sides of a wok above the water. They are available in a range of sizes.

Sweet & Sour Pork

This dish is a popular choice in Western diets, and must be one of the best known of Chinese recipes.

NUTRITIONAL INFORMATION

Calories 471   Sugars 47g
Protein . . . . .16g   Fat 13g
Carbohydrate . . .77g   Saturates 2g

🥘 10 mins   🕐 20 mins

SERVES 4

I N G R E D I E N T S

150 ml/5 fl oz vegetable oil, for deep-frying

225 g/8 oz pork fillet, cut into 1-cm/
½-inch cubes

1 onion, sliced

1 green pepper, deseeded and sliced

225 g/8 oz pineapple pieces

1 small carrot, cut into thin strips

25 g/1 oz canned bamboo shoots,
drained, rinsed and halved

cooked rice or noodles, to serve

BATTER

125 g/4½ oz plain flour

1 tbsp cornflour

1½ tsp baking powder

1 tbsp vegetable oil

S A U C E

125 g/4½ oz light brown sugar

2 tbsp cornflour

125 ml/4 fl oz white wine vinegar

2 garlic cloves, crushed

4 tbsp tomato purée

6 tbsp pineapple juice

1 To make the batter, sift the plain flour into a mixing bowl with the cornflour and baking powder. Add the vegetable oil and stir in enough water to make a thick, smooth batter (about 175 ml/6 fl oz).

2 Pour 150 ml/5 fl oz of the vegetable oil into a preheated wok and heat until almost smoking.

3 Dip the cubes of pork into the batter and cook in the hot oil, in batches, until cooked through. Remove the pork from the wok with a slotted spoon and drain on absorbent kitchen paper. Keep it warm until required.

4 Drain all but 1 tablespoon of oil from the wok and return it to the heat. Add the onion, green pepper, pineapple pieces, carrot and bamboo shoots and stir-fry for 1–2 minutes. Remove from the wok with a slotted spoon and set aside.

5 Mix all of the sauce ingredients together and pour into the wok. Bring to the boil, stirring, until thickened and clear. Cook for 1 minute, then return the pork and vegetables to the wok. Cook for another 1–2 minutes, then transfer to a serving plate and serve with rice or noodles.

Pork Chow Mein

This is a basic recipe – the meat and/or vegetables can be varied as much as you like.

NUTRITIONAL INFORMATION

Calories	239	Sugars 1g
Protein	........17g	Fat 14g
Carbohydrate	...12g	Saturates 2g

15 mins   15 mins

SERVES 4

INGREDIENTS

250 g/9 oz egg noodles

4–5 tbsp vegetable oil

250 g/9 oz pork fillet, cooked

125 g/4½ oz French beans

2 tbsp light soy sauce

1 tsp salt

½ tsp sugar

1 tbsp Chinese rice wine or dry sherry

2 spring onions, finely shredded

a few drops of sesame oil

chilli sauce, to serve (optional)

1 Cook the noodles in boiling water according to the instructions on the packet, then drain and rinse under cold water. Drain again, then toss with 1 tablespoon of the oil.

2 Slice the pork into thin shreds and top and tail the French beans.

3 Heat 3 tablespoons of oil in a preheated wok until hot. Add the noodles and 1 tablespoon of soy sauce and stir-fry for 2-3 minutes. Remove to a serving dish and keep warm.

4 Heat the remaining oil in the wok, add the French beans and the meat and stir-fry for 2 minutes. Add the salt, sugar, rice wine or sherry, the remaining soy sauce and about half of the spring onions to the wok.

5 Stir the mixture in the wok, adding a little water if necessary, then pour on top of the noodles and sprinkle with sesame oil and the remaining spring onions.

6 Serve the chow mein hot or cold, with chilli sauce if using.

COOK'S TIP

'Chow mein' literally means 'stir-fried noodles' and is highly popular in the West as well as in China. Almost any ingredient can be added, such as fish, meat, poultry or vegetables. It is very popular for lunch and makes a tasty salad served cold.

Cantonese Fried Noodles

This dish is usually served as a snack or light meal. It may also be served as an accompaniment to plain meat and fish dishes.

NUTRITIONAL INFORMATION

Calories 385	Sugars 6g	
Protein 38g	Fat 17g	
Carbohydrate . . .21g	Saturates 4g	

 5 mins   🕐 15 mins

SERVES 4

I N G R E D I E N T S

350 g/12 oz egg noodles

3 tbsp vegetable oil

675 g/1½lb lean beef steak, cut into thin strips

125 g/4½ oz green cabbage, shredded

75 g/2¾ oz canned bamboo shoots, drained

6 spring onions, sliced

25 g/1 oz French beans, halved

1 tbsp dark soy sauce

2 tbsp beef stock

1 tbsp dry sherry

1 tbsp light brown sugar

2 tbsp chopped fresh parsley, to garnish

1 Cook the noodles in a saucepan of boiling water for 2–3 minutes. Drain well, rinse under cold running water and drain thoroughly again.

2 Heat 1 tablespoon of the vegetable oil in a preheated wok or frying pan, swirling it around until it is really hot.

3 Add the noodles to the pan and cook for 1–2 minutes. Drain the noodles and set aside until required.

4 Heat the remaining vegetable oil in the wok. Add the beef and cook for 2–3 minutes. Add the cabbage, bamboo shoots, spring onions and French beans to the wok and cook for 1–2 minutes.

5 Add the soy sauce, beef stock, dry sherry and light brown sugar to the wok and stir to mix.

6 Stir the noodles into the mixture in the wok, tossing to mix well. Transfer to serving bowls, garnish with chopped parsley and serve immediately.

VARIATION

You can vary the vegetables in this dish depending on seasonal availability or whatever you have to hand – try broccoli, green pepper or spinach.

Soy & Sesame Beef

Soy sauce and sesame seeds are classic ingredients in Chinese cooking.
Use a dark soy sauce for fuller flavour and richness.

NUTRITIONAL INFORMATION

Calories	324	Sugars	.........2g
Protein	........25g	Fat	..........22g
Carbohydrate	....3g	Saturates	.......6g

5 mins   10 mins

SERVES 4

INGREDIENTS

2 tbsp sesame seeds

450 g/1 lb beef fillet

2 tbsp vegetable oil

1 green pepper, deseeded and thinly sliced

4 garlic cloves, crushed

2 tbsp dry sherry

4 tbsp soy sauce

6 spring onions, sliced

freshly boiled noodles, to serve

1 Heat a large wok or heavy-based frying pan until it is very hot.

2 Add the sesame seeds to the pan and dry-fry, stirring, for 1–2 minutes, or until they just begin to brown. Remove the sesame seeds from the wok and set aside until required.

3 Using a sharp knife or meat cleaver, thinly slice the beef.

4 Heat the vegetable oil in the wok or frying pan. Add the sliced beef and stir-fry for about 2–3 minutes or until sealed on all sides.

5 Add the sliced green pepper and crushed garlic to the pan and continue stir-frying for 2 minutes.

6 Pour the dry sherry and soy sauce into the pan and stir together. Add the sliced spring onions. Cook the spring onions in the liquid for approximately 1 minute, stirring occasionally. Let the mixture in the pan bubble, but do not let it burn.

7 Transfer the beef stir-fry to warm serving bowls and scatter with the dry-fried sesame seeds. Serve hot with freshly boiled noodles.

COOK'S TIP

You can spread the sesame seeds out on a baking tray and toast them under a preheated grill until browned all over, if you prefer.

Lamb with Mushroom Sauce

Try to use a lean cut of lamb for this simple yet delicious recipe, for both flavour and tenderness.

NUTRITIONAL INFORMATION

Calories 219   Sugars 1g
Protein . . . . .21g   Fat 14g
Carbohydrate . . . .4g   Saturates 4g

🥟 5 mins   🕐 10 mins

SERVES 4

I N G R E D I E N T S

350 g/12 oz lean, boneless lamb

2 tbsp vegetable oil

3 garlic cloves, crushed

1 leek, sliced

175 g/6 oz large mushrooms, sliced

½ tsp sesame oil

fresh red chillies, to garnish

S A U C E

1 tsp cornflour

4 tbsp light soy sauce

3 tbsp Chinese rice wine or dry sherry

3 tbsp water

½ tsp chilli sauce

1 Using a sharp knife or meat cleaver, cut the lamb into thin strips.

2 Heat the vegetable oil in a preheated wok or large, heavy-based frying pan.

3 Add the lamb strips, garlic and leek and cook for about 2–3 minutes.

4 To make the sauce, in a bowl mix together the cornflour, soy sauce, Chinese rice wine or dry sherry, water and chilli sauce and set aside.

5 Add the sliced mushrooms to the pan and cook for 1 minute.

6 Stir in the prepared sauce and cook for 2–3 minutes or until the lamb is cooked through and tender.

7 Sprinkle the sesame oil over the top and transfer the lamb and mushrooms to a warm serving dish. Garnish with red chillies and serve immediately.

VARIATION

The lamb can be replaced with lean steak or pork fillet in this classic recipe from Beijing. You could also use 2–3 spring onions, 1 shallot or 1 small onion, instead of the leek, if you prefer.

Lime Mousse with Mango

Lime-flavoured cream moulds, served with a fresh mango and lime sauce, make a stunning dessert.

NUTRITIONAL INFORMATION

Calories 254	Sugars 17g	
Protein 5g	Fat 19g	
Carbohydrate ...17g	Saturates 12g	

10 mins   0 mins

SERVES 4

I N G R E D I E N T S

250 g/9 oz natural fromage frais

grated zest of 1 lime

1 tbsp caster sugar

125 ml/4 fl oz double cream

M A N G O   S A U C E

1 mango

juice of 1 lime

4 tsp caster sugar

T O   D E C O R A T E

4 cape gooseberries (physalis)

strips of lime zest

1   Put the fromage frais, lime zest and sugar in a bowl and mix together.

2   Whisk the double cream in a separate bowl, then fold it into the fromage frais mixture.

3   Line 4 decorative moulds or ramekins with muslin or clingfilm and divide the mixture evenly between them. Fold the muslin or clingfilm over the top and press down firmly.

4   To make the sauce, slice through the mango on each side of the large, flat stone, then cut the flesh from the stone. Remove the skin and discard.

5   Cut off 12 thin slices and set aside. Chop the remaining mango, put into a food processor with the lime juice and sugar and blend until smooth. Alternatively, push the mango through a sieve and then mix with the lime juice and sugar.

6   Turn out the moulds onto serving plates. Arrange 3 mango slices on each plate, pour some sauce around and decorate with cape gooseberries and lime zest.

COOK'S TIP
Cape gooseberries have a tart and mildly scented flavour and make an excellent decoration for many desserts. Peel back the papery husks to expose the bright orange fruits.

Exotic Fruit Salad

This is a sophisticated fruit salad that makes use of some of the exotic fruits that can now be seen in the supermarket.

10 mins   15 mins

SERVES 6

I N G R E D I E N T S

3 passion fruit

125 g/4½ oz caster sugar

150 ml/5 fl oz water

1 mango

10 lychees, canned or fresh

1 star fruit

1 Halve the passion fruit and press the flesh through a sieve into a saucepan.

2 Add the sugar and water to the pan and bring gently to the boil, stirring.

3 Put the mango on a chopping board and cut a thick slice from either side, cutting as near to the stone as possible. Cut away as much flesh as possible in large chunks from the stone section.

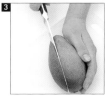  

COOK'S TIP

A delicious accompaniment to any exotic fruit dish is cardamom cream. Simply crush the seeds from 8 cardamom pods, add 300 ml/ 10 fl oz whipping cream and whip until soft peaks form.

4 Take the 2 side slices and make 3 cuts through the flesh but not the skin, then 3 more cuts at right angles to make a lattice pattern.

5 Push each piece inside out so that the cubed flesh is exposed and you can easily cut it off.

6 Peel and stone the lychees and cut the star fruit into 12 slices.

7 Add all the mango flesh, lychees and star fruit to the passion fruit syrup and poach gently for 5 minutes. Remove the fruit with a slotted spoon.

8 Bring the syrup to the boil and cook for 5 minutes until it thickens slightly.

9 To serve, transfer all the fruit to individual serving glasses or bowls, pour over the sugar syrup and serve warm.